OUR SOLAR SYSTEM

Pluto

BY DANA MEACHEN RAU

Content Adviser: Dr. Stanley P. Jones, Assistant Director, Washington, D.C., Operations, NASA Classroom of the Future

Science Adviser: Terrence E. Young Jr., M.Ed., M.L.S., Jefferson Parish (La.) Public Schools

Reading Adviser: Dr. Linda D. Labbo, Department of Reading Education, College of Education, The University of Georgia

COMPASS POINT BOOKS

MINNEAPOLIS, MINNESOTA

Compass Point Books
3722 West 50th Street, #115
Minneapolis, MN 55410

Visit Compass Point Books on the Internet at *www.compasspointbooks.com*
or e-mail your request to *custserv@compasspointbooks.com*

Photographs ©: NASA, cover, 1, 3, 8–9, 12 (all), 13, 15, 16–17; Bob Winsett/Corbis, 4; Hulton/Archive by Getty Images, 5, 7; Bettmann/Corbis, 6 (top), 20–21; Dave G. Houser/Corbis, 6 (bottom); PhotoDisc, 10–11, 22–23 (bottom), 24–25; Courtesy NASA/JPL/Caltech, 14, 22–23 (top); Roger Ressmeyer/Corbis, 18; The Johns Hopkins University Applied Physics Laboratory/Southwest Research Institute, 19.

Editors: E. Russell Primm and Emily J. Dolbear
Photo Researcher: Svetlana Zhurkina
Photo Selector: Dana Meachen Rau
Designer: The Design Lab
Illustrator: Graphicstock

Library of Congress Cataloging-in-Publication Data

Rau, Dana Meachen, 1971–
  Pluto / by Dana Meachen Rau.
    p. cm. — (Our solar system)
  Includes index.
  Summary: Briefly describes the discovery, surface features, orbit, moon, and efforts to study the planet Pluto.
  ISBN 0-7565-0297-7 (hardcover)
  1. Pluto (Planet)—Juvenile literature. [1. Pluto (Planet)] I. Title.
  QB701 .R38 2002
  523.48'2—dc21   2002002947

Table of Contents

Looking at Pluto from Earth

✦ Do you like to ice-skate? Some people skate on ice rinks. Others skate on lakes or ponds. Imagine a skating pond as large as a whole planet! That may be what the icy surface of Pluto looks like.

Most of the planets in the solar system are very big. Jupiter, the largest planet, could hold almost 1,400 Earths. Pluto is the smallest planet. It is smaller than the continent of North America. It is even smaller than seven of

Parts of Pluto may be covered with ice, ▶
like a frozen pond in winter.

the moons in the solar system. The moons Io, Europa, Ganymede, Callisto, Titan, Triton, and Earth's moon are all bigger than Pluto.

Pluto is hard to see in the night sky. It can be seen only with a very large telescope. Even through a telescope, Pluto looks just like another star. No wonder it was hard to find.

An astronomer named Percival Lowell studied Uranus and Neptune. He thought the seventh and eighth planets moved in a strange way. He believed

◀ *Percival Lowell (1855–1916) began the search for a ninth planet.*

there might be a ninth planet pulling on them. So he tried to figure out where this new planet would be.

After he died, a young astronomer named Clyde Tombaugh continued the search. He worked at the Lowell Observatory in Arizona. He pointed a camera at the sky near where he thought the planet might be. Then he took pictures one to two weeks apart. He was looking for something that moved against the back-ground of stars. Finally, he found a "dot" that seemed to

Clyde Tombaugh (1906–1997) studied ▶ *the sky at the Lowell Observatory in Arizona (bottom).*

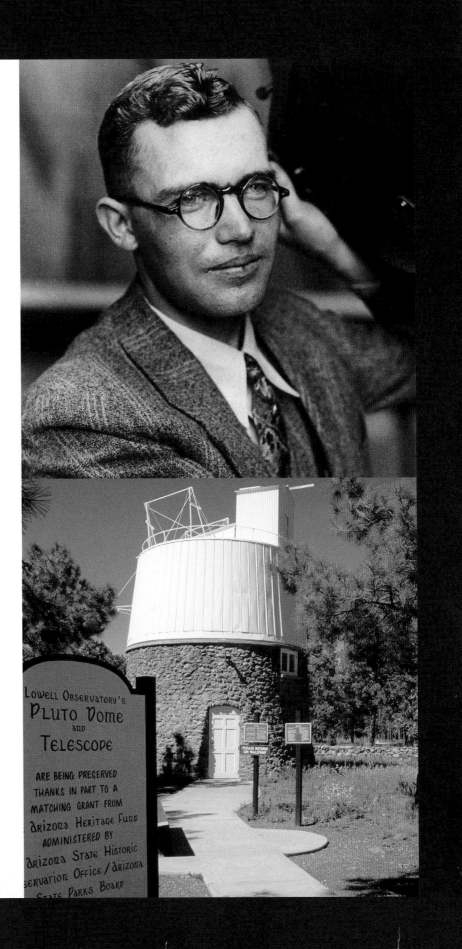

LOWELL OBSERVATORY'S
PLUTO DOME
AND
TELESCOPE

ARE BEING PRESERVED
THANKS IN PART TO A
MATCHING GRANT FROM
Arizona HERITAGE FUND
ADMINISTERED BY
Arizona STATE HISTORIC
SERVATION OFFICE / Arizona
STATE PARKS BOARD

move. That "dot" turned out to be a new planet. He discovered it in 1930.

At first, people didn't know what to name the planet. Eleven-year-old Venetia Burney in Oxford, England, thought of the name *Pluto.* Pluto was the Roman god of the underworld. She thought it would be a good name for the planet, because it was so dark and so far away. Other people liked the name, too, because the first two letters of *Pluto* are Percival Lowell's initials.

The planet Pluto was named after the Roman god of the underworld. ▶

Looking at the Way Pluto Moves

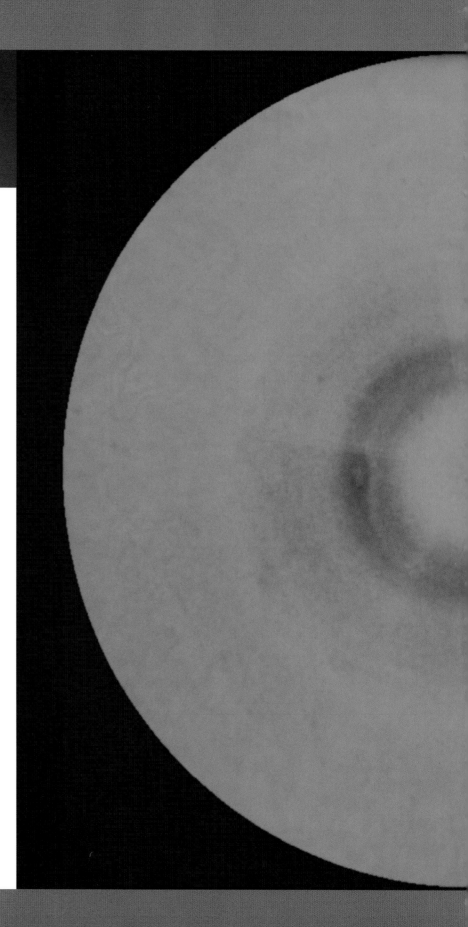

All nine planets travel around the Sun, or revolve, in paths called orbits. One trip around the Sun is a planet's year. Pluto is far away from the Sun, so its trip takes a very long time. It takes Pluto almost 248 Earth-years to revolve. Planets also spin, or rotate, as they revolve. One rotation is a planet's day. Pluto rotates slowly. It takes Pluto more than six Earth-days to spin once.

The orbits of the planets

Sometimes Neptune, not Pluto, is the ▶
farthest planet from the Sun.

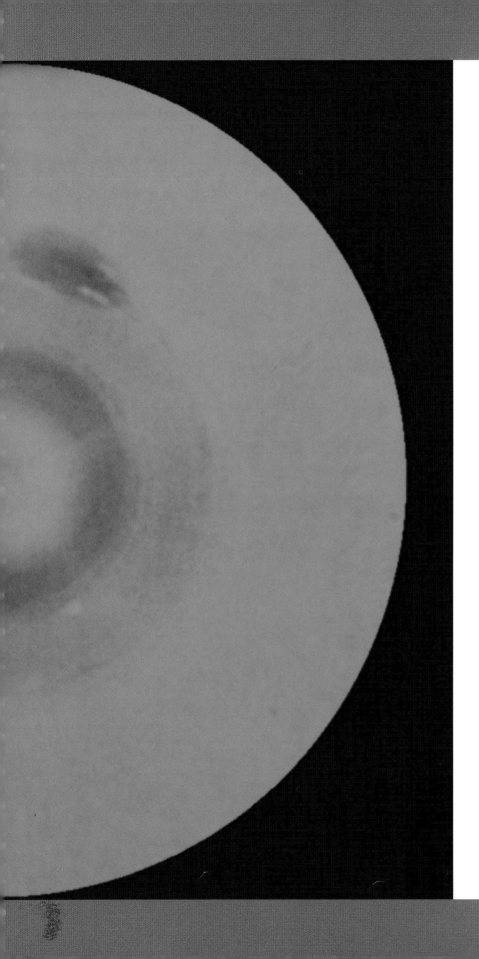

are elliptical or oval-shaped. Pluto's is the most oval orbit of all. Sometimes it even comes inside the orbit of Neptune. When this happens, Pluto is actually closer to the Sun than Neptune is. Then Neptune, not Pluto, is the farthest planet from the Sun. This happens only for 20 years of its almost 248-year orbit. Pluto was the eighth planet and Neptune was the ninth from 1979 to 1999. Now Pluto is back to being the ninth planet for about the next 228 years.

Looking Through Pluto

✦ The first four planets from the Sun are Mercury, Venus, Earth, and Mars. They are called the rocky planets. That is because they are made up mostly of rock. The next four planets are Jupiter, Saturn, Uranus, and Neptune. They are called gas giants. They are very large and made up mostly of gases. Pluto is different from all the other planets.

Scientists believe Pluto is made up mainly of rock and

◀ *From right to left: Mercury, Venus, Earth, and Mars are rocky planets. Jupiter, Saturn, Uranus, and Neptune are gas giants. Pluto is unlike all of them.*

ice. If you could cut Pluto in half and look inside, there might be a rocky **core** in its center. The core is surrounded by water ice.

Pluto's surface looks reddish. It has some bright areas and some dark ones. Scientists think the light areas are ice. The dark areas may be made of rock. The top and bottom of the planet are called **poles**. Pluto may have large white areas of ice called **ice caps** on its poles.

Above Pluto's surface is

▲ *Pluto has a reddish surface. Temperatures on Pluto are a very cold average of –373°F (–225°C).*

◄ *Scientists believe the light areas on Pluto are ice. The dark areas may be rock.*

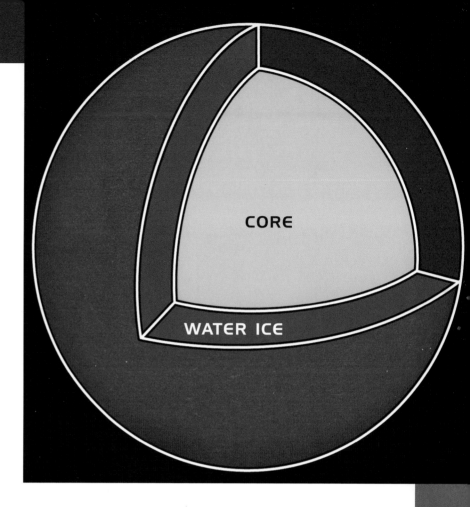

CORE

WATER ICE

its atmosphere. An atmosphere is made up of the gases around a planet. Pluto's atmosphere changes all the time. Pluto's oval orbit means that sometimes it is very close to the Sun. Other times it is very far away. When Pluto is close to the Sun, the gases of the atmosphere float around the planet. But when Pluto moves away from the Sun, the gases freeze. They fall down on the planet like snow. The planet is covered with frost. Pluto doesn't really have an atmosphere during this part of its year.

Pluto's temperature changes, too. It is warmer on Pluto when it is close to the Sun. It is colder when Pluto is far away from the Sun. Pluto's average temperature is –375 degrees Fahrenheit (–225 degrees Celsius).

Looking Around Pluto

✦ Pluto has one moon named Charon. Earth only has one moon, too. But Pluto and Charon are very different from our Earth and its moon.

American astronomer James Christy discovered Charon in 1978. That is almost fifty years after Pluto was discovered. For a long time, telescopes were not strong enough to see the planet. As telescopes became more powerful, they could see more. At first, Christy thought

The same sides of Pluto and Charon ▶
always face each other.

Pluto was pear-shaped. Then he figured out that there was a moon next to Pluto. Charon is about half the size of Pluto.

Charon does not orbit around Pluto the way other moons orbit their planets. Charon and Pluto orbit each other. They circle each other with the same side always facing the other. It is like they are playing ring-around-a-rosy. Some people think of Pluto and Charon as a kind of double planet, rather than as a planet and a moon.

▼ *Some people call Pluto and Charon a double planet.*

Looking at Pluto from Space

Astronomers often send spacecraft into space to study planets more closely. Pluto is the only planet that has never been visited by spacecraft. Scientists learn about Pluto from their telescopes on Earth. They also look at pictures of Pluto taken by the Hubble Space Telescope. The Hubble Space Telescope is a very large telescope that orbits in space. It takes pictures and sends them back to computers on Earth.

The Hubble Space Telescope orbits the Earth. It can take pictures of objects far away in space. ▶

Astronomers want to send a spacecraft to Pluto. It is called *New Horizons*. A launch is planned in 2006. It will not reach Pluto for about ten years after that.

The spacecraft will fly by the planet and take pictures and gather facts. It will answer questions about the surfaces of Pluto and Charon and what they are made of.

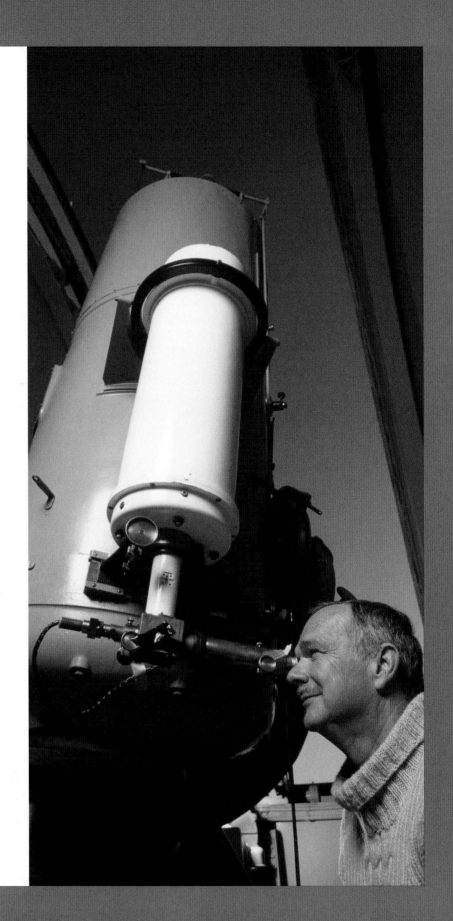

Even with strong telescopes on ▶ *Earth, Pluto is hard to see.*

The planned mission of New ▶▶ Horizons *will finally answer many questions scientists have about Pluto.*

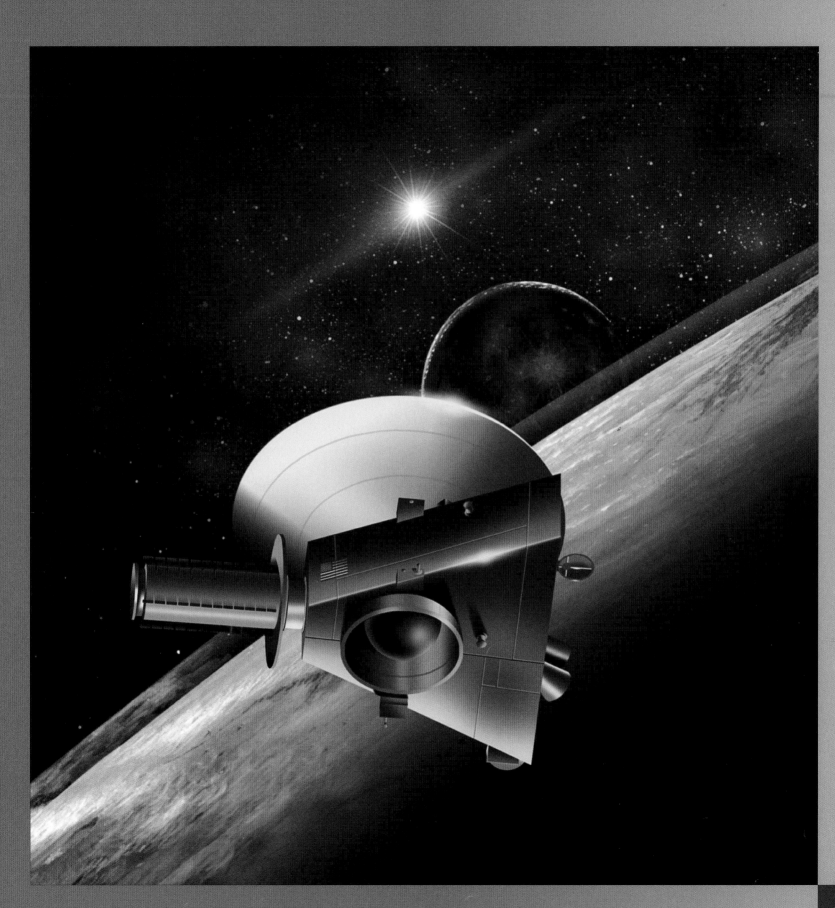

Looking Beyond Pluto

⋆ *New Horizons* won't end with Pluto, however. It will go past Pluto to the Kuiper Belt. The Kuiper Belt is an area beyond Pluto that is filled with pieces of rock and ice. The spacecraft will reach the Kuiper Belt around 2026. The Kuiper Belt was named for Gerard Kuiper (1905–1973). He was a famous astronomer who studied the objects orbiting the Sun beyond Pluto.

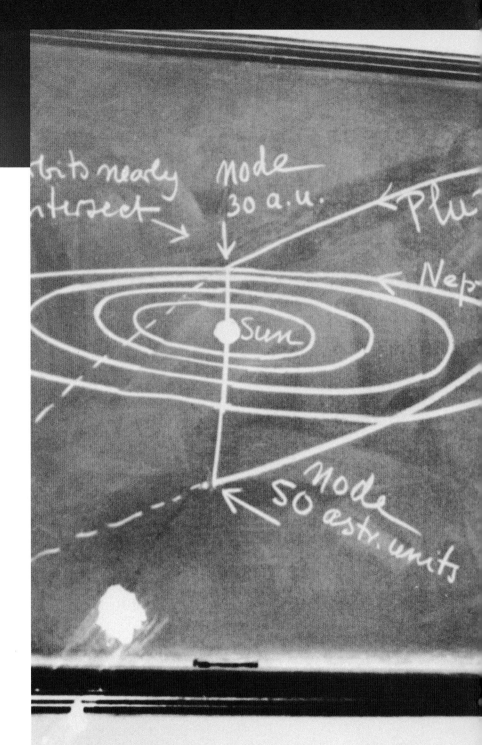

Gerard Kuiper explains his ideas about ▸
Pluto and objects orbiting the Sun
beyond it.

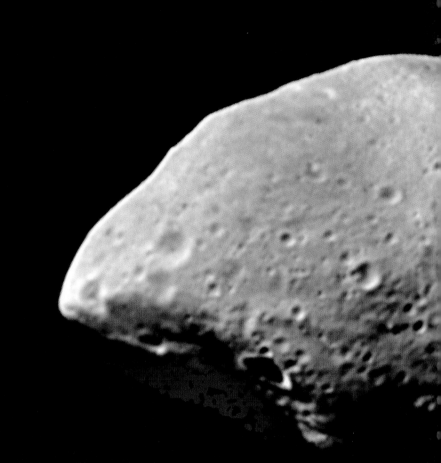

Some scientists call these pieces of rock and ice "mini-planets." Like Pluto, they are very far from the Sun and very cold. Scientists believe some objects in the Kuiper Belt may be as large as Pluto and Charon.

Looking to the Future

⋰⋱ Scientists think the solar system began as a spinning cloud of gases and dust around the Sun. Some of the gas and dust clumped together. These clumps became the planets. They think Pluto formed in a different way because it is so different from all the other planets. They think it may have come from the Kuiper Belt. Or it may be a smaller piece of ice and rock, such as an

◀ *Some people don't believe Pluto should be called a planet. They think Pluto is more likely an asteroid (above) or a comet (below).*

asteroid or a **comet**. Or it may have been a moon of Neptune that escaped from its orbit.

Scientists have many questions about Pluto. They want to know why Pluto is so small, so far from the Sun, and so different from the other planets. Some people don't even think Pluto should be called a planet! Perhaps a mission to Pluto will give us the answers to these questions and many others.

Pluto is so far away from Earth that it ▶
may always be a mystery.

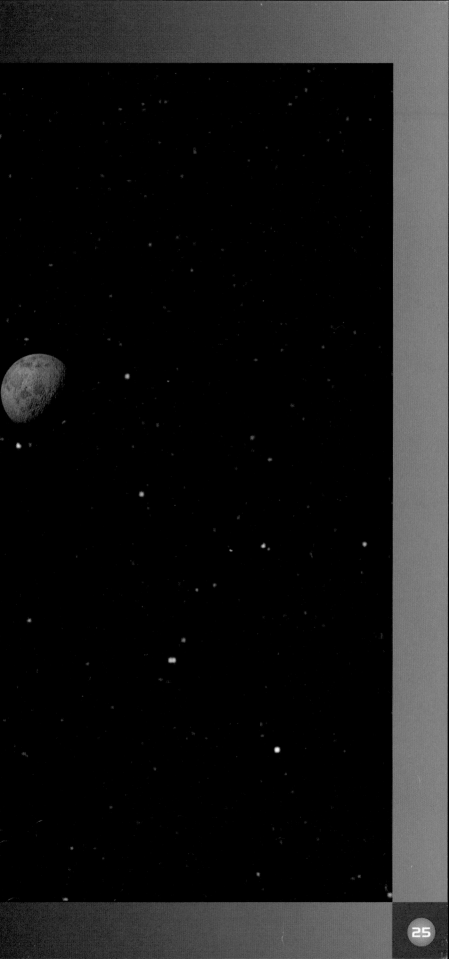

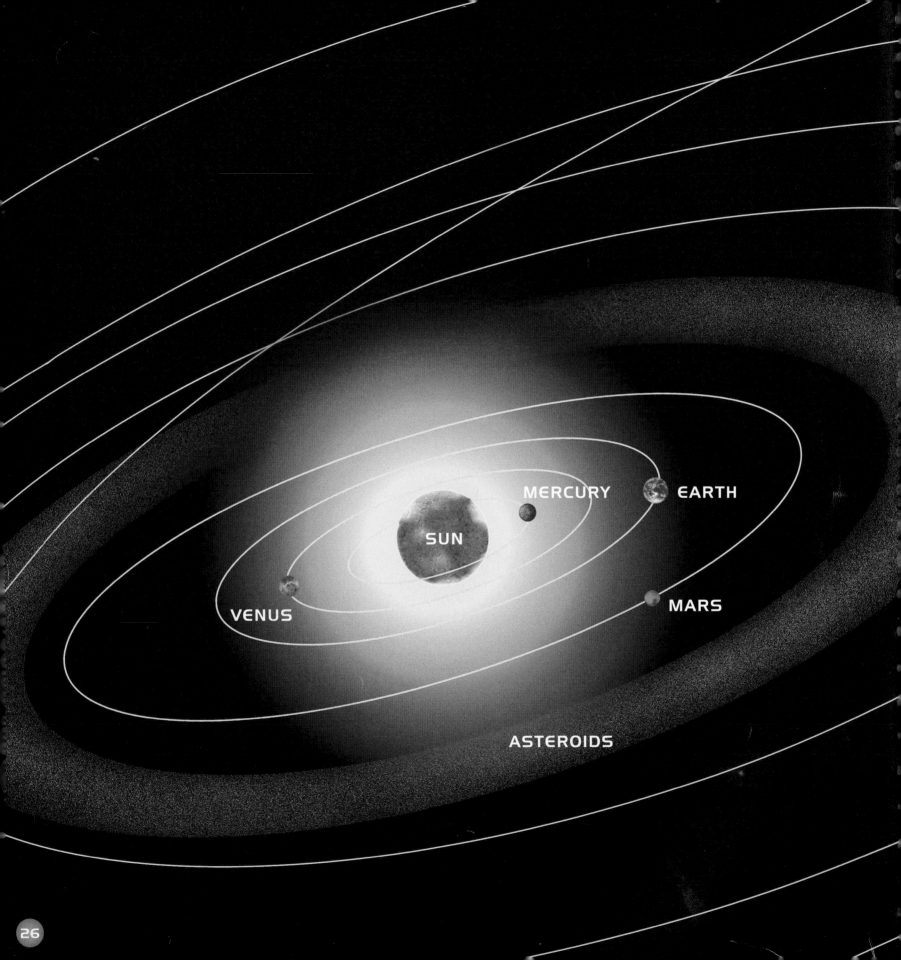

SUN

MERCURY

EARTH

VENUS

MARS

ASTEROIDS

JUPITER

URANUS

SATURN

NEPTUNE

PLUTO

Glossary

asteroid—a chunk of rock that orbits the Sun especially between the orbits of Mars and Jupiter

astronomer—someone who studies space

comet—a piece of ice and rock that has a long tail of dust and orbits the Sun

continent—a large land area on Earth

core—the center of a planet

ice caps—large areas of ice and snow

poles—the northernmost and southernmost points on a planet

solar system—a group of objects in space including the Sun, planets, moons, asteroids, comets, and meteoroids

telescope—a tool astronomers use to make objects look closer

temperature—how hot or cold something is

A Pluto Flyby

Pluto is the smallest planet and the farthest planet from the Sun.

If you weighed 75 pounds (34 kilograms) on Earth, you would weigh 5 pounds (2.2 kilograms) on Pluto.

Average distance from the Sun: 3,700 million miles (6,000 million kilometers)

Distance from Earth: 2,669 million miles (4,294 million kilometers) to 4,682 million miles (7,533 million kilometers)

Diameter: 1,485 miles (2,390 kilometers)

Number of times Pluto would fit inside Earth: 151.5

Did You Know?

- Pluto is the only planet discovered in the twentieth century.

- Pluto is the only planet discovered by a scientist from the United States.

- *New Horizons* will take about ten years to get to Pluto.

- Some scientists believe there is still a tenth planet to be discovered. They call it Planet X.

- Scientists think Charon has a large core, similar to Pluto's.

Time it takes to orbit around Sun (one Pluto year): 248 Earth-years

Time it takes to rotate (one Pluto day): 6.4 Earth-days

Structure: rocky core, layer of water ice

Average surface temperature: –375° Fahrenheit (–225° Celsius)

Atmosphere: nitrogen, methane

Atmospheric pressure (Earth=1.0): unknown

Moons: 1

Rings: 0

Want to Know More?

AT THE LIBRARY

Bredeson, Carmen. *Pluto*. Danbury, Conn.: Franklin Watts, 2001.

Kerrod, Robin. *Uranus, Neptune, and Pluto*. Minneapolis: Lerner Publications, 2000.

Mitton, Jacqueline, and Simon Mitton. *Scholastic Encyclopedia of Space*. New York: Scholastic Reference, 1998.

Redfern, Martin. *The Kingfisher Young People's Book of Space*. New York: Kingfisher, 1998.

Ridpath, Ian. *Stars and Planets*. New York: DK Publishing, Inc., 1998.

ON THE WEB

Exploring the Planets: Pluto
http://www.nasm.edu/ceps/etp/pluto/
For more information about Pluto

The Nine Planets: Pluto
http://www.seds.org/nineplanets/nineplanets/pluto.html
For a multimedia tour of Pluto

Solar System Exploration: Pluto
http://sse.jpl.nasa.gov/features/planets/pluto/pluto.html
For more information about Pluto and its features

Space Kids
http://spacekids.hq.nasa.gov/
NASA's space-science site designed just for kids

Space.com
http://www.space.com
For the latest news about everything to do with space

Star Date Online: Pluto
http://www.stardate.org/resources/ssguide/pluto.html
For an overview of Pluto

Welcome to the Planets: Pluto
http://pds.jpl.nasa.gov/planets/choices/pluto1.htm
For pictures and information about Pluto

THROUGH THE MAIL

Goddard Space Flight Center
Code 130, Public Affairs Office
Greenbelt, MD 20771
To learn more about space exploration

Jet Propulsion Laboratory
4800 Oak Grove Drive
Pasadena, CA 91109
To learn more about the spacecraft
missions

Lunar and Planetary Institute
3600 Bay Area Boulevard
Houston, TX 77058
To learn more about Pluto and
other planets

Space Science Division
NASA Ames Research Center
Moffet Field, CA 94035
To learn more about Pluto and
solar system exploration

ON THE ROAD

**Adler Planetarium and
Astronomy Museum**
1300 S. Lake Shore Drive
Chicago, IL 60605-2403
312/922-STAR
To visit the oldest planetarium
in the Western Hemisphere

***Exploring the Planets* and
*Where Next Columbus?***
National Air and Space Museum
7th and Independence Avenue, S.W.
Washington, DC 20560
202/357-2700
To learn more about the solar system
at this museum exhibit

**Rose Center for Earth and
Space/Hayden Planetarium**
Central Park West at 79th Street
New York, NY 10024-5192
212/769-5100
To visit this new planetarium and
learn more about the planets

UCO/Lick Observatory
University of California
Santa Cruz, CA 95064
408/274-5061
To see the telescope that was used to
discover the first planets outside of
our solar system

Index

◄ **About the Author:** *Dana Meachen Rau loves to study space. Her office walls are covered with pictures of planets, astronauts, and spacecraft. She also likes to look up at the sky with her telescope and write poems about what she sees. Ms. Rau is the author of more than seventy-five books for children, including nonfiction, biographies, storybooks, and early readers. She lives in Burlington, Connecticut, with her husband, Chris, and children, Charlie and Allison.*